THE GEMINUS

A PLAY BY
ROSS DINWIDDY

THE GEMINUS

A PLAY BY
ROSS DINWIDDY

BASED ON THE NOVELLA
THE SECRET SHARER
JOSEPH CONRAD

DARE DEVIL

BLUE DEVIL
PRODUCTIONS

bluedeviltheatre.co.uk

THE GEMINUS

First staged at The Rialto Theatre, Brighton on the 8th May 2019, with the following cast.

George Hotson ...... John Black
Leggatt ...... Gareth Wildig
Ma Gwen...... Christine Kempell
Frizer .... Ben Baeza
Skeres .... Robert Cohen

Directed by Ross Dinwiddy
Produced by Rich Bright

Blue Devil Productions

Act One - Scene One

ABOARD THE GEMINUS

A SCHOONER ANCHORED IN THE GULF OF SIAM

A ship's bell chimes 3 times and the lights go up.

***George Hotson** (The Captain),* ***Skeres** (The Chief Mate) and* ***Frizer** (The Second Mate) are sitting around a table.*

Hotson is a clean cut, young man in his late-twenties.

Skeres is the oldest of the group, with a grey beard and a weathered face.

Frizer is also a young man, about the same age as Hotson.

Hotson stands out, as he is dressed in sharply pressed trousers, a clean short-sleeved shirt and a well-tailored waistcoat. The other two are far more unkempt.

They are all eating lumpy, beige stew from battered, enamelled bowls using tarnished, old spoons.

Frizer This climate's too hot to stomach this bloody bilge.

Skeres Be grateful to God there's still food left.

Frizer But for how long? Stuck here without so much as a breeze.

Hotson glances at Skeres and Frizer.

Hotson Did you know that there's another ship anchored just inside the islands?

Skeres News to me, Captain. Haven't seen another ship in days.

Hotson There is. I could just make out her mastheads above the ridge as the sun went down.

Frizer *(With a sarcastic tone and knowing smile)* Well, I'll be damned, sir! You don't say!

Skeres studies Frizer's face for a moment. He drops his spoon into his bowl and takes out a small snuff tin. He taps out a little snuff onto his hand and snorts it deeply.

Skeres In that case, she'll be a ship lately arrived from her homeland. Doubtless she'll have drew on too much water to cross the bar. She might had made it had it been the top of the spring tide, but not now. A captain seasoned to these waters would know to make for that natural harbour marked by the great Paknam Pagoda and wait a few days, too risky to stick it out in open sea with all that water in her. That'll be it, mark my words now.

Frizer *(With a smug, matter of fact tone)* That's so. She draws over twenty feet. She's a schooner from Tiger Bay, The Sephora, with a cargo of coal from the Gorki. Hundred and twenty-three days from Cardiff.

Hotson and Skeres react with surprise and curiosity.

Frizer pauses for a moment, clearly enjoying their reaction. Then…

Frizer Tugboat skipper told me all about it when he came on board for your letters, sir. He's expecting to tow the old Sephora onto the river Meinam the day after tomorrow. There'll be good money in it for him.

Skeres Other souls far from home. At least we aboard the Geminus are on our way back.

At this, Frizer drops his spoon and gets to his feet.

Frizer Perhaps they've a Captain that knows his ship and the sea, they may be home before us yet.

Frizer abruptly walks away from the table and exits.

Hotson lowers his eyes to his bowl.

Skeres *(Clears his throat)* Who can account for that young fellow's whims? I can't for the life of me understand why he didn't just tell us the whole story straight off.

Hotson I can understand the men's patience wearing thin. They've had plenty of hard work on this voyage and precious little time off. Now they find themselves caught in this dead calm with me, a replacement captain they barely know.

Skeres Not for me to say, sir.

Hotson stirs his stew languidly with his spoon.

Hotson Tell all hands that I won't set an anchor watch tonight. I'll keep deck myself.

Skeres *(Clearly surprised and puzzled but trying not to show it)* Very well, sir. You know best, I'm sure.

Hotson makes for the door, but Frizer is on his way back in. They pass awkwardly as Hotson exits.

Frizer How did we get stuck with him?

Skeres He means well enough. And he'll be taking the anchor watch himself tonight. Alone too, by the sound of it. That's something.

Frizer plonks into the seat where Hotson had sat.

Frizer What you saying, a Captain taking an eight hour watch himself whilst we do nothing? I don't believe it.

Skeres It's true, he just told me.

Frizer Well, more fool him. But anyhow, me and the men will be making the most of that. Happen he just wants to get used to actually having a deck under his feet. It'll be a novelty for him.

At this they both chuckle.

Lights snap to blackout.

Act One - Scene Two

THE QUARTER-DECK OF THE GEMINUS

The light is low, but with a blue and slivery glimmer. There is the sound of the gentle lapping of the sea.

Skeres stands with an oil lamp in his hand.

Hotson wanders onto the deck, also with an oil lamp. He is dressed in dove grey, silk pyjamas with a pair of burgundy Grecian slippers. The pyjama jacket is unbuttoned.

Skeres You'll be all right on your own tonight, Sir?

Hotson *(Feeling patronised)* Perfectly. Are you joining the other men now, Skeres?

Skeres That sort of revelry is not exactly my kind of thing, sir. Leave it to the youngsters, I say. I'm off to my bunk.

Hotson Goodnight, Skeres.

Skeres hmm…

Skeres exits.

Having watched Skeres go, Hotson begins pacing the deck looking around with the aid of the lamp. He pauses and takes a pocket watch from his pocket, he checks the time, then goes back to pacing the deck.

There is a rope ladder stretching from the stage up the central aisle, through the audience. Hotson spots it and hurries towards it.

Hotson *(Muttering to himself)* Why on earth has this not been wound in?

As Hotson takes hold of the ladder, a bare chested man appears from the back of the theatre, he walks until he stands near the other end of the ladder. This is **Leggatt** *– He is about Hotson's age, perhaps a little younger and very handsome indeed. He is soaking wet, his skin and hair glisten in the bluish, silvery light.*

Hotson sees Leggatt, narrows his eyes, then takes a few steps forward.

Hotson Hello down there. What's the matter?

Leggatt Cramp. *(Beat)* I say, no need to call anyone.

Hotson I wasn't about to.

Leggatt Are you alone on deck?

Hotson Quite alone. Yes.

Leggatt smiles. Silence.

Hotson Look, don't swim away just yet!

Leggatt I don't intend to, yet. *(Beat)* What's the time?

Hotson The time? A few minutes after midnight.

Leggatt I suppose that means that your captain's turned in for the night?

Hotson I'm sure he hasn't.

Leggatt *(Dropping his head down and muttering with frustration)* Oh, what's the good?

Hotson Is there anything I can do?

Leggatt Look here. Is there any way you could possibly call the Captain out quietly for me?

Hotson I am the captain.

Leggatt *(Almost to himself)* Are you now? *(Then with a warm smile)* My name's Leggatt.

Hotson Hello, Leggatt. My name's George Hotson. You must be a good swimmer.

Leggatt Yes, I am and I'm most pleased to meet you, George Hotson. I've been in the water since nine o'clock. The question for me now is whether I go on swimming 'til I sink from exhaustion, or *(Beat)* come on board here.

They exchange a smile and then Leggatt begins to walk towards the stage, treading carefully between the rungs of the ladder. As he reaches the stage we see that he is only dressed in wet, white shorts.

Hotson *(Taking Leggatt by the arm and helping him onto the ship)* What's happened?

Leggatt An ugly business.

Silence for a moment, then…

Hotson And?

Leggatt *(Pointing back out over the audience)* You can't see it but there's a ship over there.

Hotson Yes, I know. The Sephora. Did you know anything of us?

Leggatt Hadn't the slightest idea. I'm the mate of her… *(Pause)* Or should I say, I was the mate.

Hotson Something's wrong?

Leggatt Yes. Very wrong indeed. I've killed a man.

Hotson What do you mean? Just now?

Leggatt No, on the passage. Weeks ago. Thirty-nine south. When I say a man…

Hotson Fit of temper?

Leggatt does not answer.

Hotson frowns.

Hotson Let me get you something to put on, then we'll decide what we're going to do next. Stay here.

Hotson turns his back, his expression sombre, full of thought. He makes for below deck and exits.

A moment later, Frizer appears.

Leggatt immediately spots Frizer and ducks out of sight.

Frizer crosses the stage unaware of the hiding stranger in the shadows.

Hotson returns carrying another set of pyjamas, identical to the one he is wearing.

The sound of merriment and camaraderie is coming from below deck - laughing, singing, raised voices in chattering high spirits. Hotson pauses for a moment and listens.

Frizer reappears carrying two bottles of rum, one in each hand. He heads in the direction of the merriment. He pauses for a moment and silently watches Hotson, who is unaware of his presence. A knowing and somewhat condescending smile develops on Frizer's face.

Frizer Not in your nice tailoring tonight, Sir?

Hotson *(Startled at first but quickly collects himself.)* It's this blasted heat. I find this more comfortable.

Frizer Forgive my ignorance. Is that what a gentleman wears in hot weather these days?

Hotson No, this is just my night suit.

Frizer Oh, I see. Would that be silk?

Hotson Umm... I think so.

Frizer *(Looking Hotson up and down.)* Yes, it's silk all right. My girl back in England is fond of fine nightwear too. She's nothing so elegant as that though, sir. I'd wager she'd give her ten pretty little toes for a nightie made of silk like that.

Hotson Well, you're in the right part of the world. Perhaps you can take her home some Siam silk.

Frizer Perhaps I will. You have a lady waiting for you, sir?

Hotson No. No, I don't.

Frizer gives a 'thought so' smile and raises the two bottles of rum.

Frizer Better be getting back to the other men.

He swaggers off and exits.

Hotson watches him go with a look of serious contemplation on his face. He turns to see Leggatt cautiously raising from his hiding place. Hotson stares at Leggatt for a moment, then walks slowly towards him. A warm smile grows on Hotson's face.

Hotson *(Reaching Leggatt)* Here, put these on.

Hotson hands Leggatt the pyjamas, who immediately turns his back, takes off the wet shorts and begins to change into the pyjamas.

Leggatt *(As he dresses, occasionally glancing over his shoulder at Hotson)* My father's a parson in Carmarthen. Do you imagine me before a judge and jury on a charge like this? As far as I'm concerned, I can't see the point. There are fellows that are angels sent from heaven – but I'm not one of them. The chap I killed was one of those creatures that are constantly simmering with a sort of stupid, self-serving wickedness. Destructive devils that have no entitlement to live at all. He wouldn't do his duty and he wouldn't let anybody else do theirs. Puts us all at risk. But what's the good of talking! You must know the sort of ill-conditioned snarling cur...

Hotson *(Interrupting)* Yes, I think I know this sort of character and I know that dealing with them is near enough impossible.

Leggatt is now dressed in the identical dove grey, silk pyjamas, he too has left the jacket unbuttoned. He and Hotson stand like mirror images of each other in the low, shimmering light.

Leggatt It happened while we were setting a reefed foresail, at dusk. A reefed foresail! The only sail we had left - so you can imagine what the horrendous weather had been like for days. I knew it might be the only thing that could save us. Then, right in the midst of this, he gave me some more of his blasted insolence. I tell you, I was at breaking point with that horrible storm, which by then seemed to have no end. Horrible, I tell you. Horrible. I think the fellow himself was half crazed, believing that he and all those around him would soon be dead. Well, that presumption turned out to be only partially true. *(Beat)* For me, the time for any gentlemanly rebuke was over, *(He raises a fist and shakes it)* I turned round and felled him like an ox. But he was soon up and at me with both fists flying. We closed in on each other just as the most terrible sea yet made for the ship like an all-consuming avalanche.

Hotson I can see it, as if I were there myself.

Leggatt All hands saw that monstrous wave coming at us and took to the rigging, but I had him firmly by the throat, and went on shaking him like a rat, the men above us yelling, 'Look out! look out!' Then there was a crash as if the heavens had fallen and the heavens were made of rock.

Leggatt and Hotson step a little closer together, they are now less than a foot apart.

Leggatt For over ten minutes, hardly anything could have been seen of the ship, just three masts driving along in a smother of foam. When the crew found me, I was still gripping the man by the throat. His face was so purple it looked almost black, his eyes like the white of an egg and ready to burst. I'd pressed my fingers so deeply into his flesh as to have hands sodden with his blood. The sight was too much for the men. It seems they rushed us aft together, still gripped as we were. They were screaming 'Murder! Murder!' like a bunch of lunatics, with the ship still running for her life.

Hotson What about your captain?

Leggatt Oh, the skipper, too, was raving like the rest of them. They'd all been deprived of sleep for more than a week, and to have this sprung on them at the height of that furious gale could have drove anyone out of their mind. I wonder they didn't fling me overboard after getting the carcass of their precious shipmate prised from my bloody grip. *(Beat)* They had the devil's own job to separate us, I've been reliably informed.

Leggatt examines Hotson's still, yet thoughtful face.

Leggatt You see, a sufficiently fierce story to make a dusty old judge and a respectable British jury sit up and take notice. The first thing I heard when I came to myself was the maddening howling of that endless gale, then the voice of the skipper. 'Mr. Leggatt, you have brutally killed a man. You can no longer act as chief mate of this ship.' *(He shrugs)* A rather superfluous assertion, I would have thought.

The crew's singing and merriment suddenly becomes even louder. A door creaks. There are footsteps.

Hotson attempts to block any sight of Leggatt with his body, he has a worried expression.

Hotson We'd better slip down to my stateroom. And

please, be as quiet as you possibly can.

They silently walk off together.

Lights snap to blackout.

Act One - Scene Three

THE CAPTAIN'S STATEROOM

Hotson lights an oil lamp as the stage lights go up. The room is shadowy, with a faint orange glow.

Leggatt *(Studying the room)* Are we safe here?

Hotson I think so. Unfortunately that door can't be locked, but nobody should enter without knocking and getting my permission. It'll be all right… I think. But for the meantime, at least, you won't be able to leave this stateroom.

Leggatt Don't concern yourself, I'm used to it. I've spent the last seven weeks locked in a cabin less than half the size of this one.

Leggatt wanders over to a desk with some papers spread out on the surface. He glances at them and then turns back to Hotson.

Leggatt This has all been a pretty thing to have to own up to for a Conway boy.

Hotson You're a Conway boy?

Leggatt I am *(He taps a finger on one of the papers)* I see you are too.

Hotson I don't remember ever seeing you there.

Leggatt Nor I you.

Hotson *(Almost to himself)* I suppose you could have already graduated by the time I joined.

Leggatt *(Blankly)* Yes, that would explain it.

Hotson hands Leggatt a towel, who begins drying his hair.

Hotson *(Watching Leggatt closely)* How did you come to be hanging onto our side ladder? For a moment there, I took you for a naked corpse adrift in the water.

Hotson get a bottle of Scotch and two glasses.

Leggatt Well, by the time we sighted Java Head, I'd had plenty of time to contemplate escape. Almost six weeks of doing little else. I reckoned by nightfall we'd have reached the Sunda Straits – there the coast would be within two or three miles. I've won a prize or two for swimming in my time, the first in my second year at Conway. I knew I could make it.

Hotson hands Leggatt a drink.

Hotson I suppose you were considering breaking through the door and effecting your escape once dark.

Leggatt No. With all the unavoidable noise, there'd have been an immediate rush to stop me and I certainly wasn't going to break out only to get chucked back. The only result would have been a violent struggle. Somebody else might have got killed.

Hotson So what was your plan?

Leggatt I asked to speak to the skipper. He always seemed sick when he came to see me, unable to even look me in the face. Anyway, he came. I can see him now, glaring at me as if I had the hangman's noose round my neck already. I asked him right away to leave my cabin door unlocked at night. Told him that the confinement was detrimental to my health and that a stroll on deck, at my leisure, would be of great benefit to me.

Hotson (*Narrowing his eyes in disbelief*) Did he go for that?

Leggatt (*Shaking his head*) He refused, looking more sick than ever. But not for fear that I'd make an escape. The reason he gave was for the safety of the men. The safety of the men!

Hotson *(Thoughtfully)* I see.

Leggatt You'd have thought they were afraid I'd go about strangling people in their beds. Am I a mad murdering brute? Do I look it? If I had been, he wouldn't have trusted himself like that into my room, alone.

Hotson He's a seasoned captain, he must surely be something of a courageous man.

Leggatt Him, 'A courageous man!' He's afraid of his own crew, he's afraid of that second mate of his for a start, a grey-headed old humbug. And he's afraid of his steward, too. A dogmatic loafer who hated me like poison from the day we set sail, just because I was the chief mate. No chief mate ever made more than one voyage on the Sephora, you know. Come to think of it, God only knows what the skipper isn't afraid of. The little nerve he did have went to hell in a handcart the night of that blasted storm. Then there is that wife of his. Oh, yes! That old witch is on board too. They say she married him to take charge of a ship. No women in the merchant navy, that's the rules. Rubbish, I know one who's the real captain of her own ship. Ma Gwen, they call her.

Leggatt drains his glass.

Hotson *(Taking the glasses and pouring them both*

another drink) This is all most curious. But none of it explains how you came to be clinging to our rope ladder in the middle of the night.

Leggatt *(With a subtle smile)* I'm getting to it. We dawdled our way through the Java Sea; drifted aimlessly about Carimata for most of the last week. So frustrating... But then we anchored here.

Hotson *(Returning with the refilled glasses)* But you're still locked in your cabin.

Leggatt Yes, in the end getting free turned out to be a rather simple affair. Earlier tonight that steward brought me my supper. As he left, there was no double clunk from the latch. So I knew immediately that he'd forgotten to lock the door. I gave it a moment or two and simply strolled out onto the quarter-deck. There was no one about. I remember thinking that I really could use the fresh air and the exercise - the confinement had indeed been detrimental to my health. I don't know what else I was thinking but next I found myself kicking off my shoes and diving into the water. Somebody must have heard the splash. They soon raised an awful hullabaloo. 'He's gone! Lower the boats! He's committed suicide! No, he's swimming.' Certainly, I was swimming. It's not so easy for a swimmer like me to commit suicide by drowning. I heard them pulling about in the dark, hailing this way and that. Then everything seemed to quieten down. I was well clear of the ship and I wasn't going back.

Hotson What happened to your clothes?

Leggatt First chance I had, I took them off and left them to drift. If they found them, let them think what they liked. Perhaps that would be suicide enough. I meant to swim 'til I sank or found land. I swam for what must have been a mile or so, then rested, clinging to a rock in the sea. Everything about was as still as death. It was from there that I first spotted your riding light – it must have been about another mile off at least.

Hotson So you swam for our light?

Leggatt Straight for it. It was at last something to swim for. For over an hour I hadn't seen a single star in the sky and I certainly hadn't seen any land. The water had been like an eternal mirror reflecting nothing but blackness. I'd been suspended and lost in a void, terrified by the notion that I was careering round and round like some crazed bullock near death. Perhaps I'd been heading back, I didn't know. Imagine if after all this, me being hauled from the sea by the scruff of the neck by my shipmates and having to fight like a wild beast? Somebody would have got killed for certain, and I didn't want any more of that. But now I'd seen a distant light and it brought me to your ladder.

Hotson When you reached it, what were you expecting to…?

There is a knock at the cabin door

Leggatt reaches out and touches Hotson lightly on the shoulder.

Hotson Duck out of sight.

Leggatt puts down his glass and stands so as to be obscured when the door is opened.

Hotson waits until Leggatt is in place, nods at him and then opens the door.

Frizer is standing there.

Frizer I noticed you weren't on deck, *(Beat)* Sir.

Hotson *(Nervous)* Did you? I shan't be long, I just needed… *(He collects himself)* Anyway, time you were getting yourself to your bunk, Frizer. I'll need you with a clear head to square the yards by lifts and braces before the other hands go to breakfast.

Frizer *(Somewhat taken aback)* Yes, Sir.

Hotson Now run along. It's late.

Hotson does not wait any longer, he closes the door with Frizer still standing there.

Leggatt *(Whispering)* He couldn't have heard us talking, could he?

Hotson *(Also whispering)* I hope not.

Leggatt Who was that?

Hotson My second mate, Frizer.

They move back to centre stage and resume talking at a normal volume.

Leggatt What sort of a chap is he?

Hotson I don't know much about him. That was the first practical order I've given the man.

Leggatt You've only lately taken charge here?

Hotson I was appointed captain of the Geminus when I least expected anything of the sort, not quite a fortnight ago. I don't yet know either the ship or her crew. I hadn't the time in port to look about her or size anybody up. And as to the crew, all they know of me is that I've been assigned to take the ship home. For the rest, I am almost as much of a stranger on board as you are. And at this moment I feel it most acutely. We'll have to tread carefully, you and I, it won't take much to make me a suspect person in the eyes of most of them.

They are again standing like mirror images of each other at centre stage.

Leggatt Then we'll tread carefully.

Leggatt reaches out and briefly yet firmly touches Hotson on the upper arm.

Hotson Leggatt, so you'd reached the ladder, but you didn't call out or attempt to draw attention to yourself in anyway.

They sit down on the bed.

Leggatt Your ladder, who'd have thought of finding a ladder hanging over the side of an anchored ship, out here, at night! I was just becoming faint when I reached it. I wasn't even capable of swimming round as far as your rudder chains. And, lo and behold there was a ladder to get hold of. After I gripped it, I said to myself, 'What's the good?' When I saw a man's head looking over I thought I would try to swim away and leave him shouting after me. I didn't mind being looked at. I - I liked it. And then there was you speaking to me so quietly, as if you'd expected me, that made me hold on a little longer. It had been a confounded lonely time. I don't mean while swimming. I was glad to talk a little to somebody that didn't belong to the Sephora. I don't know - I wanted to be seen, to talk with somebody, right then. To talk to and be seen by you.

Hotson Well, you did ask for the captain.

Leggatt *(With a deep yawn)* That was just an impulse. It would have been of no use really, with my pursuers pretty certain to be round here by sometime tomorrow.

Hotson *(Distracted)* Do you really think the Sephora's crew will come... tomorrow?

Leggatt Quite likely.

Leggatt yawns again and stretches.

Hotson *(Getting to his feet)* Hmm. We shall see then. Meantime get yourself into this bed and get some sleep.

Leggatt puts down his empty cup and lies back on the bed resting his head on the pillow.

Hotson *(Pulling a sheet over Leggatt's body)* I should be getting back to my watch. Good night, Leggatt.

There is no answer, Leggatt is already asleep.

Hotson looks at him for a moment, then heads for the door. As he goes, he glances back and...

Lights snap to blackout.

Act Two - Scene One

THE CAPTAIN'S STATEROOM

The room is as before, but the light is now brighter with a warm yellow glow.

Hotson is at his desk writing with a beautiful, gold nib fountain pen. He is still in his pyjamas but now the buttons of the jacket are done up.

Leggatt is asleep in the bed.

There is a knock at the door.

Hotson *(Calling out)* One moment!

Hotson gets up and goes over to open the door. Once it is opened, we see Frizer standing there. Hotson holds the door to block any view of the bed.

Frizer Beg pardon, sir…

Hotson Well…

Frizer There's a ship's boat heading our way, sir.

Hotson All right. Get the ladder over.

Hotson closes the door. He goes over to the bed, rests a hand on Leggatt's shoulder and shakes him gently.

Leggatt's eyes open and he springs up into a seated position.

Leggatt What's happened?

Hotson Nothing yet, but it sounds as if the Sephora's long boat is pulling up alongside as we speak.

There is another knock on the door. Hotson again goes over to answer it.

Leggatt jumps out of bed and into a nearby recess.

Hotson opens the door, it is Frizer again.

Hotson Yes?

Frizer Excuse me, sir, but I forgot to take your tray. *(Muttered under his breath)* Or wasn't given a chance.

Hotson glances over his shoulder, Leggatt is well out of sight.

Hotson It's over there on the desk.

Frizer Thank you, sir.

Frizer goes to collect the tray.

Hotson backs into a position that is between the desk and where Leggatt is hiding. He keeps his eyes firmly on Frizer.

Skeres enters, a bit breathless.

Skeres Sir, that ship's boat is from The Sephora. Someone calling themselves Ma Gwen is coming aboard now.

Hotson narrows his eyes.

Hotson I've heard of Ma Gwen. I think we can be confident that she speaks for the Sephora's captain in whatever matter has brought her here.

Frizer exits with the tray. He seems to glance suspiciously at Hotson as he goes.

Skeres *(After a few tuts)* A lady holding authority on a British ship…

Hotson Yes, that's what I understand and…

Skeres *(Interrupting)* …and now she's come here. *(He shakes his head)* I gave the permission to come aboard, sir. Assumed it would be all right, with you giving the order to put the ladder out and all.

Hotson Of course it's all right. Escort the lady straight to me.

Skeres Yes, sir.

Skeres exits muttering very quietly to himself, we may just be able to make out...

Skeres *(Mumbled whisper)* And we think we've got it bad.

Hotson dashes over to where Leggatt is hiding.

Hotson Stay hidden, Leggatt. Your Ma Gwen is here and on her way down now.

Leggatt *(Whispered)* Oh, no. I'll be like the grave.

Hotson hurriedly rearranges the chairs near the desk. He positions one with its back to Leggatt's hiding place and tosses a damp towel over the it. He sits in the other chair, which faces it.

Just as he sits, there is a knock at the door.

Hotson Enter!

Skeres enters, closely followed by Ma Gwen.

Skeres Ma Gwen of The Sephora to see you, sir.

Skeres loiters, eyeing Ma Gwen with a bemused frown.

Hotson *(Standing)* Your reputation precedes you, madam. *(Beat)* I'm very pleased to meet you.

Ma Gwen Likewise.

They shake hands, Hotson seems a little surprised by the firmness of her grip.

Hotson I'm Captain Hotson. Please have a seat.

Hotson picks up the damp towel and indicates the chair

Ma Gwen *(Sitting down)* Don't mind if I do.

Hotson then notices the loitering Skeres…

Hotson That will be all, Skeres

Skeres *(As if snapping out of a daze)* Pardon me?

Hotson I said, that will be all.

Skeres Oh…

Skeres wanders out, closing the door behind him with a clunk.

Hotson tosses the damp towel aside.

Hotson Do excuse the mess, we weren't expecting company and I've just been performing my ablutions.

Hotson returns to his chair.

Hotson Now, what can I do for you?

Ma Gwen Plenty, I hope.

Ma Gwen takes a thin, black cheroot from a case and lights it.

Hotson *(Indicating a bottle of rum on the desk)* May I offer you a drink?

Ma Gwen Thank you, no. I never take liquor. Never! I will have some water, though.

Hotson pours a tumbler of water from a carafe. Ma Gwen drinks it straight down and then holds out the glass to be refilled without saying a word.

Hotson pours her another glass.

Ma Gwen Terrible thirsty work. From the crack of dawn, I've been exploring the islands round here about. Well, I say islands, nothing more than lumps of rock, most of them.

Hotson What was that for, fun?

Ma Gwen Fun! No! Duty, painful duty.

Hotson I'm terribly sorry. But can I ask you to speak up a bit? *(He glances towards where Leggatt is* *hiding)* I'm a little hard of hearing. It's an annoying affliction, but there you are.

Ma Gwen Hard of hearing you say? And in such a young man, too! What was the cause of it, some disease I expect?

Hotson Yes; disease. Anyway, what brings you to the Geminus.

Ma Gwen I'm searching for a killer, that's what I'm doing. Our Chief Mate is the wanted man, he wrung the neck of another able-bodied seaman. It happened at the height of a storm too, the like of which I've never seen. Coming down like cobblers it was and the breaking waves were even worse. That night my Chief Mate was supposed to give me a reefed foresail, but he handed me a murdered shipmate into the bargain. I've had him under lock and key for weeks, but he got loose last night and swam for it.

Hotson Gracious.

Ma Gwen What would you think if such an atrocity were to happen on your ship? I've run the Sephora for these past fifteen years. I am as well-known and respected as any captain. Been at sea since I first posed as a cabin boy, seven-and-thirty years ago, and I've never heard of such a thing happening on a British ship. And that it should be on my ship. And with my frail husband on board, too. He's a delicate man, sir. The whole affair has turned him bilious. What a predicament.

Hotson Are you certain of your Chief Mate's guilt? Have you entertained the idea that with the sea the way you say it was, it might have been some sort of accident? I've heard tales of the sheer weight of a wave killing a man very neatly, by simply breaking his neck.

Ma Gwen Good God! The sea! No man killed by the sea ever looked like that.

Ma Gwen breaths in and raises her eyebrows.

Ma Gwen If you'd seen that sight, you'd have never forgot it for as long as you lived. *(She nods slowly)* The weather was too bad to give the corpse a proper, Christian, sea burial. So next day, at dawn, we took it up on the poop and covered its face with a bit of my best bunting. I read a prayer - 'Blessed are the Poor in Spirit', dammed good one that and short with it. And then, just as it was, in its oilskins and long boots, we launched it amongst those mountainous seas that still seemed ready to swallow up my ship and all the desperate souls on board her.

Hotson I'd say, that reefed foresail saved you.

Ma Gwen Under God, it did. It was by a very particular and divine mercy we lived through those hurricane squalls, I firmly believe that.

Hotson But the setting of that sail must have…

Ma Gwen I say God's own hand was in it. Nothing less could have delivered us from that cold inferno. I might have given the order, but I take no credit now!

Hotson Your order?

Ma Gwen That it was.

Hotson takes a cigarette from his case and lights it.

Hotson So you're very anxious to find your mate, and ultimately, give him up to the authorities?

Ma Gwen I am that, we can't be seen to be countenancing any doings of that sort. Seven-and-thirty virtuous years at sea, I've had. The last fifteen of them on the Sephora - Immaculate command though sacred wedlock. I see it as my sworn duty to hold a pitiless obligation. A pitiless obligation to the law of men and angels.

Hotson I'm certain, that your handling of this unfortunate situation will only enhance your reputation.

Ma Gwen It's very good of you to say so. *(Beat)* Do you know, we did not engage that young fellow ourselves, my husband and I. We were in a way forced to take him on. Forced. His people have some sort of interest with our owners. He was always very well turned out – dapper you might even call it, and all highly decorous in his way of speaking. But I never took to him. I'm a woman who appreciates plainness. You see, he wasn't exactly the right sort for chief mate of a ship like the Sephora. No, I never took to him.

Ma Gwen stubs out her cheroot.

Hotson Too much of a gentleman for this sort of work?

Ma Gwen Some might say that, he was all very la-di-da when he wanted to be. But 'Leggatt the Savage', the men called him, and that's what he turned out to be.

Hotson What are you going to do now?

Ma Gwen Seein' as you aboard the Geminus know nothing, I suppose I must report a suicide.

Hotson I beg your pardon?

Ma Gwen Suicide! That's what I'll have to write to our owners directly I get back

Hotson Unless you manage to recover him before tomorrow, alive, I mean.

Ma Gwen Tomorrow! Alive! The land, I say, the mainland is at least seven miles off my anchorage.

Hotson About that.

Ma Gwen He's a strong man and fit as a fish in the water, but I still can't see him thrashing his way through seven miles of open sea. *(Thoughtfully, and getting to her feet)* But I reckon I had no more than a two-mile pull to your ship though. Not a bit more. Not a bit more.

Hotson And quite enough, too, in this awful heat.

Ma Gwen is pacing the room, glancing round inquisitively.

Hotson *(Also getting to his feet)* Nice little stateroom, isn't it?

Ma Gwen Not so little.

Hotson And very well fitted out, too. There's a handsome washroom in that alcove, which I've just been availing myself of.

Ma Gwen Yes, it all looks highly convenient and comfy with it.

Ma Gwen prods at the bed, still glancing round.

Hotson Perhaps you'd like a look round?

Ma Gwen Ordinarily, I'd love to. Make for a pleasant and diverting conversation with my husband. Though he is prone to rabid jealousy and excessive sulking in his weakened state, so best not…

Hotson Are you certain I can't tempt you. The saloon too is impressively appointed.

Ma Gwen You do make it all sound very tempting, but sadly, no. I'm a woman with urgent business. A killer to catch or write off as dead.

Hotson Another time perhaps. In which case, I'll get one of the men to see you to your boat. It does seem like a suicide we're looking at here.

Ma Gwen Happen the sea herself has been his hangman. And that would make it God's work, a divine execution. I'd be satisfied with that.

Hotson and Ma Gwen make for the door. Hotson leads the way.

Ma Gwen has one last glance round.

Hotson has already opened the door for her.

Frizer and Skeres are just outside, they step into the room and stand alongside Hotson.

Ma Gwen goes to exit, but turns and…

Ma Gwen I say… you… you don't think that…

Hotson glances nervously at Frizer and Skeres then back to Ma Gwen with a broad, forced smile.

Hotson *(Loudly and cupping his right ear with his hand)* Certainly not.... I'm delighted. Goodbye. Skeres, see Ma Gwen to her launch.

Skeres Yes, sir.

Ma Gwen frowns, shakes her head and shrugs.

Ma Gwen *(With disdain)* Disease! And in such a young man, too! *(She turns and continues to walk)* Judge not the Lord by feeble sense, but trust him for his grace.

She and Skeres exit.

Frizer looks more than a little confused at this, he gives Hotson a very perplexed look. Then…

Frizer I wouldn't feel comfortable taking orders from a woman. No way!

Hotson *(Returning to the desk)* Wouldn't you?

Frizer Don't seem right. Can't be right. (Beat) Her crew told our chaps one hell of a story, if it's true. I suppose you had it all from the lady there, sir?

Hotson Yes. I got a story from her.

Frizer drops into a chair.

Frizer A very horrible affair, isn't it, sir?

Hotson It certainly sounds it.

Frizer Right up there with all these tales we hear about grisly murders on Yankee ships. Beats them too, you might say.

Hotson I don't think it resembles them in the slightest.

Frizer *(Sarcastically)* I've not much acquaintance with American ships, not I, so I won't go against your vast knowledge. What I've been told today is plenty horrible enough for me... But the queerest part is that those fellows seemed to have some notion that the man is hidden aboard here. They had really. Did you ever hear of such a thing?

Hotson Preposterous.

Frizer There was something of a quarrel about it. Our chaps took offence. 'As if we'd harbour a man like that,' they said. 'Wouldn't you like to look for him in amongst our cargo, down there with all the rice and spice? Or perhaps we've got him dressed up as our Captain.' Beg your pardon about that one, sir. It was all quite a tiff. But they made it up in the end. I suppose he did drown himself. Don't you, sir?

Hotson *(Attempting to sound stern)* I don't suppose anything. Of course he did.

Frizer You have no doubt in the matter, sir?

Hotson None whatever. Anyway, I've been distracted by this ugly business long enough. *(He nods at the desk)* I've work to do.

Frizer We all have, sir. And now it looks like the wind is picking up and we must take advantage of that. We wouldn't want to be stuck here much longer.

Hotson *(Softly, to himself)* No, we wouldn't.

Frizer exits.

Leggatt emerges from the alcove.

Hotson Did you manage to hear any of that?

Leggatt All of it – you being hard of hearing was an inspiration.

Hotson Thank you.

Leggatt The bloody charlatan told you she gave the reefed sail order.

Hotson *(Distracted, not looking at Leggatt)* Yes, but attributed the ship's salvation to god's hand.

Leggatt I assure you she never gave the order. She may think she did, but she never gave it. She stood there with me on deck, just after the main topsail blew away, and didn't have a clue what to do. And with the night and the storm coming on like hungry jaws! To have no leadership in such a crisis was enough to drive any man out of his mind. It worked me up into a sort of wild despair. I was boiling, furious… *(Beat)* Feral. But what's the use telling you? You know! You must know!

Hotson *(Thoughtfully)* Had you lost your temper with the men before this, Leggatt?

Leggatt Do you think that if I hadn't been pretty fierce with them from time to time I should have got them to do anything? No! And that night it was a hundred-fold the challenge - we weren't so much confronted with a heavy sea, as a sea gone mad! The elements gone insane. Having seen that night, I think I now know what the end of the world will look like.

Hotson I think I understand.

Leggatt *(Touching Hotson gently on the arm)* I need you to, George.

They make firm eye contact and hold it for a few moments. Then Hotson suddenly becomes uncomfortable.

Hotson *(Breaking away)* You must be hungry.

Leggatt *(Beat)* Famished.

Hotson produces a box filled with cans. He starts to take them out and line them up on the desk.

Hotson Stashed away for an emergency. Pate de Foie Gras, asparagus, turtle soup, cooked oysters and perhaps a little less luxurious, pilchards. All manner of abominable sham delicacies out of tins. You're welcome to them all. I should also be able to get you morning coffee and nightly rum without arising suspicion. Bread too. Can you think of anything else that you're going to need?

Leggatt Well, I can think of a number of things. But for now, *(Picking up a tin of oysters)* a tin opener, would be handy.

Hotson produces a tin opener from the box and places it on the desk triumphantly.

Leggatt picks it up. He glances between the tin and the opener, then back to Hotson.

Hotson *(Heading for the door)* Enjoy your oyster breakfast. Take a deep breath of sea air from the porthole and try to imagine they're fresh. I do need to show my face on deck now. The wind seems to have returned and she might be ready to drag us away from here. *(Exit)*

Leggatt watches him go with a contemplative expression, then he drops the tin and tin opener onto the table.

Lights snap to blackout

Act Two - Scene Three

THE CAPTAIN'S STATEROOM

The lights are low, warm and cosy. An empty rum bottle sits on the desk. Hotson and Leggatt are drinking.

Hotson At first, I thought I'd be able to pass you off as a new sailor as soon as we got to a port or anywhere else to take on supplies. That was the plan I was developing.

Leggatt And it's a good one. We should do it.

Leggatt drains his glass and puts it down.

Hotson Impossible, now. Since Ma Gwen's visit, the whole crew seem to have an explicit description of you. You've been quite the topic of conversation amongst the men for days. They'd know instantly who you really are… or suspect, at least.

Hotson drains his glass and puts it down too. The gesture is remarkably similar to Leggatt's.

Leggatt So we must carry on as we are.

Hotson Yes, all the horrible manoeuvring, all the miserable juggling with the unavoidable.

Leggatt My nerve's been tested to the limit.

Hotson Really? You always appear perfectly self-controlled, more than calm - almost invulnerable.

There is a sharp knock at the door. Hotson winks at Leggatt who quickly and silently dashes over and presses his back to the wall, just where the open door will conceal him.

Hotson answers the door - it is Frizer who is holding two bottles of rum..

Frizer hands Hotson the bottles.

Frizer Little party for one tonight is it, sir?

Hotson *(Bored and dismissive)* That'll be all, Frizer

Frizer shrugs and leaves.

Leggatt steps from his hiding place, just as Hotson tosses the door shut.

Hotson puts one bottle on the desk and begins opening the other.

Hotson I've started to hate the sight of that man. Not because of remarks like that one. I've started to hate his very presence here. Perhaps his whole existence. Is that wrong of me?

Hotson pours them both a large rum.

Leggatt Not in the slightest. I've heard enough from the man myself to hate him as if he were nothing but a festering infection.

Hotson I've come to hate many things since the beginning of our secret partnership. All the things that have stood against us. The silence of the ship when we're whispering to one another at night. I hated the stillness of the air and the calm water about us, at least that's changed now and we're on the move. But I still feel myself resenting the elements, the men, time…

Leggatt *(Thoughtfully)* Time. It's certainly not our friend in this.

Hotson I'm taking us through the Eastern side of the Gulf of Siam. The most direct and fastest route, but also the most risky. There's no population nearby to speak of, no tug boats to bring us even the most meagre of supplies. If the wind fails us for a sizable length of time here and I don't know what would get us first, starvation or the inevitable mutiny. Possibly some devilish combination of both.

Leggatt You're making the right choices, George, the bold choices. Don't doubt your resolve now.

Hotson For the first time, I'm experiencing the feeling of a ship moving under my feet, guided by my own independent word. *(He smiles at Leggatt warmly, then chuckles softly)* But I know I'm not wholly alone in my command - for there is a secret sharer hidden in my cabin.

Leggatt You're the captain of this ship. You alone.

Hotson Am I? I sometimes have the feeling of being in two places at once. It's affected me physically and mentally. It's almost as if your presence here is soaking into my soul.

Leggatt gazes into his glass of rum for a moment.

Leggatt I understand what you mean, I feel it too.

The lights snap to blackout.

Act Three - Scene One
THE CAPTAIN'S STATEROOM

The light is again low and warm, as if the room is only lit by oil lamps. But now the sound of the beating rain and the howling wind outside comes from all around.

Leggatt crosses the stage, he is shirtless and has a towel over his arm. He disappears into the alcove with the washroom.

There is a knock at the door. Beat. Another knock.

Skeres enters carrying a long oilskin coat. He glances around, he looks a little confused. The door is left wide open as Skeres also crosses the stage and disappears into the recess where the washroom is.

A moment later, Skeres reappears without the coat and walks back across the stage.

As Skeres reaches the halfway point, Hotson enters.

Hotson is now dressed in boots, a shirt and white trousers.

Hotson *(Startled, supressed panic)* What on earth are you doing in here, Skeres?

Skeres Brought your long oilskin down, sir.

Hotson Was that really that necessary?

Skeres *(Confused)* Knew you'd be needing it with the weather being the way it's been these past four days, sir, ever since the wind picked up we've…

Hotson *(Looking round anxiously)* What have you done with it?

Skeres The lining still needed drying, sir. I've hung it in your washroom there.

Hotson The washroom? I see. That'll be all. And, Skeres, don't come barging in here again when I'm not about.

Skeres That's the funny thing, sir. I could have sworn I heard you in here.

Hotson Did you knock?

Skeres I did.

Hotson And did I say 'enter'?

Skeres Of course not. You were…

Hotson Exactly, you're imagining things, man. Don't let this happen again.

Skeres *(Raises his eyebrows and puffs)* Sorry, sir.

Skeres exits shaking his head contemptuously.

Hotson breaths a deep sigh of relief, but then suddenly starts to look round again, anxious.

Hotson Leggatt? Leggatt?

Leggatt emerges from the alcove, his body and hair are wet, he is dressed only in a towel, hitched round his waist.

Hotson *(Relieved)* You're still here.

Leggatt I was taking a bath.

Hotson But he didn't see you.

Leggatt He knocked the outer door and I thought nothing of it. But then I heard footsteps in here heading my way. *(Beat)* I managed to squat myself under the water, just in time.

Hotson Under the water? *(With disbelief in his voice)* And that was sufficient?

Leggatt The fellow only opened the door and put his

arm in to hang the coat up. All the same…

Hotson *(Blurted out)* I thought I'd lost you.

Leggatt No. *(He smiles and puts his arms around Hotson's waist)* You haven't lost me.

Hotson glances at Leggatt's hands, he seems a little confused. Then he looks back into his face.

Leggatt suddenly pulls Hotson close and kisses him passionately on the mouth. The kiss lasts for a few seconds, then Hotson pushes him away.

Hotson You shouldn't have done that.

Leggatt cups his hand over his mouth and nose then breaths sharply into it, as if checking for bad breath.

Leggatt *(Jovially, unfazed)* You're the one who's been feeding me pilchards.

Hotson You know what I mean.

Hotson turns and walks away from Leggatt.

Hotson You've made a mistake about me.

Leggatt Have I?

Hotson *(With his back still turned)* There was a tugboat skipper that called on us with supplies when we were stuck in that dead calm. He was quite chummy with Frizer. I know he also visited the Sephora, he even towed them onto the Meinam a few days ago.

Leggatt Is that right?

Hotson turns back to face Leggatt.

Hotson Yes. He was bound to have told someone on the Sephora about The Geminus. And I can easily imagine him talking about me and men like Frizer's opinion of me too.

Leggatt Umm, I'd say that was more than likely.

Hotson Yet, when you arrived, you told me you knew nothing of The Geminus and me.

Leggatt And that was true. Believe it or not, they didn't bother to keep their caged killer up to date with every bit of gossip they hear.

Hotson If you say so. *(Almost to himself)* You can't stay in this cabin forever.

Leggatt I know. Even you won't be in this room forever. Time….

Hotson Yes, time. I'll be heading for England and I imagine that's the last place you'd want to end up.

Leggatt There or any of her colonies.

Hotson Agreed and it would never do for you to come to life again.

Leggatt The answer's simple, you must maroon me as soon as we get amongst the islands off the Cambodge shore.

Hotson Maroon you! We're not living in some boy's own adventure tale.

Leggatt We aren't indeed! There's nothing of a child's story in any of this. But there's nothing else for it. I want no more. I must face some sort of justice. I've always been judged by people who are fond of quoting the Bible, well, what does the Bible say? 'Driven off the face of the earth.' That's penance fit for Cain. Very well, I'll be off the face of the earth - gone. As I came at night so I shall go.

Hotson Impossible! You can't.

Leggatt Can't I?

Hotson Stop it!

Leggatt Not naked like a soul on the Day of Judgment. I shall be shrouded in your sleeping suit.

Hotson Now I know you're not being serious.

Leggatt I've never been more so.

Hotson Oh, for heaven's sake! When?

Leggatt Perhaps the Last Day is already upon us.

Hotson drops his head and angrily mutters something incomprehensible to himself, then he takes a deep breath and...

Hotson It can't possibly be done now. The ship's on the off-shore tack and, as you know, the wind may fail us yet.

Leggatt It may, it may not.

Hotson You're an impossible man, Leggatt. *(Beat)* Look, tomorrow night there may be a chance. If you keep insisting on this madness.

Leggatt *(Moving in close to Hotson, making firm eye contact.)* I can do it, I can face it, as long as I know that you understand me, really understand me. *(Beat)* But of course you do. You've been my second self. It's been a great satisfaction to have had somebody who understands. You seem to have been put here on purpose. This has all been very wonderful.

Hotson seems to think for a moment but maintains solid eye contact with Leggatt. Then, he suddenly clasps his arms around Leggatt's body, pulls him close and kisses him on the lips. This is a strong yet relatively brief kiss.

Hotson draws his head back, he looks nervous, his lower lip trembling.

They hold eye contact for a moment, then both men move in on each other and begin kissing passionately.

After a few seconds, they part and stand back, they now move in perfect unison, as if mirror images of each other.

Leggatt starts unbuttoning Hotson's shirt.

Hotson looks anxious, startled, but allows Leggatt to carry on undressing him. Once the shirt is removed, they start kissing again.

Leggatt unbuttons Hotson's trousers as they kiss.

Hotson pulls away Leggatt's towel. They fall onto the bed, kissing and caressing each other.

Lights snap to blackout

Act Three - Scene Two

THE CAPTAIN'S STATEROOM

The rain has stopped. The light is brighter now, as if the morning sun is streaming through the portholes.

Leggatt's head stirs on the pillow, then he sits up in bed and stretches.

Hotson stands at the desk, a towel is hitched round his waist. He is diligently studying a large chart using a brass magnifying glass.

Leggatt *(Yawning)* Come back to bed.

Hotson *(Not looking away from the chart.)* There's nowhere I'd rather be, but right now I'm attempting to save your life. *(He puts down the magnifying glass and seems to think for a second)* Do you still intend to leave?

Leggatt Yes, I must. For both our sakes. Please don't try to stop me.

Hotson That's what I thought you'd say. *(Glances at the chart then looks back to Leggatt)* Well, you know, I don't think you have to be marooned after all.

Leggatt I've no confidence of finding anywhere but a barren island within swimming distance. One day, perhaps, I'll see life again, but for the meantime marooned is the best I can expect.

Hotson I think that's where you're wrong.

Hotson takes the chart over to the bed. He sits on the edge and spreads the chart out between them. They both lean over the large sheet of paper.

Hotson This whole area is not well charted, but, there… *(He points)* That's got to be Koh-ring. I've been studying this map all morning. Look, it's got two hills and a low point. You see. It has to be inhabited. And on the coast opposite there is what looks like the mouth of a biggish river, with some towns, most likely, not far up. It's the best chance for you that I can see.

Leggatt Anything. Koh-ring let it be.

Leggatt looks thoughtfully at the chart, then puts an arm around Hotson's shoulders.

Leggatt We two are giants looking down on this land and this sea from a lofty height. In charge of all we survey. *(He runs a finger along the chart)* From there it wouldn't take much to go wandering onto this blank land of Cochin-China, and then… *(He* *runs his finger further, right off the edge of the paper.)* Off the face of the earth.

Hotson The Geminus will clear the south point as she heads now. Goodness only knows when, though, but certainly it will be sometime after dark, tonight. I'll edge her in to half a mile, perhaps less, as far as I may be able to judge in the dark.

Leggatt Be careful, George - your future, the only future you may have, would be in ruins if any disaster befell your first command.

Hotson I know, but I'm confident that I can do it. I must do it.

There is a knock at the cabin door.

Hotson *(Calling out, but casually with no panic in his voice)* One moment.

Leggatt gets up, hitches another towel round his waist and dodges into the alcove.

Hotson quickly returns to the desk.

Hotson Enter!

Skeres and Frizer enter.

Frizer slouches and yawns insolently.

Hotson Aren't you properly awake yet?

Frizer Yes, sir! I'm awake.

Hotson Well, then, be good enough to hold yourself as if you are, man! I'll be needing you to keep a close lookout today and into the night too.

Frizer stands up straight and clears his throat.

Frizer Yes, sir. Sorry, sir.

Hotson I'm going to stand right in. Quite in - as far as I can take her.

Skeres and Frizer exchange a quick, worried glance.

Hotson We're not doing too well out here in the middle of the gulf. I'm taking The Geminus in to look for the land breezes. We'll start now and keep that course right through the night.

Skeres Bless my soul! Do you mean, sir, in the dark amongst all them shoals and jagged rocks and reefs?

Hotson Well, if there are any regular land breezes at all on this coast one must get close inshore to find them, mustn't one?

Skeres *(This time under his breath)* Bless my soul!

Hotson And Frizer, I want you and a couple of

hands to open the two quarter-deck ports.

Frizer Open the quarter-deck ports! What for?

Hotson The only reason you need concern yourself about is because I tell you to do so. Have them open wide and fastened properly. Understood?

Frizer Yes, sir.

Hotson Now run along the both of you, I'll have more orders once I'm dressed and on deck. It's going to be an important twenty-four hours for us all.

Skeres and Frizer exit. Once the door is closed behind them, Leggatt emerges from the alcove.

Hotson There are a few more things I need to explain. Once I go on deck today, we'll have precious little time left together.

Leggatt *(Dropping onto the bed)* I know.

Hotson *(Walking back to the bed)* As I say, I shall take her in as close as I dare and then put her round.

Leggatt reaches out, takes Hotson by the hand and pulls him onto the bed next to him.

Hotson I'll find a way to smuggle you out of here and into the sail locker, which communicates with the lobby. When all the hands are aft at the main braces you'll have a clear road to slip out and get overboard through the open quarter-deck port. I've had them both fastened up. Use a rope's end to lower yourself into the water so as to avoid a splash. A splash might be heard by the men and that would only complicate matters.

Leggatt studies the map for a few more moments in silence.

Hotson watches him intently.

Leggatt *(Softly)* I understand.

Hotson takes hold of Leggatt by the shoulders and looks deep into his eyes.

Hotson I won't be able to be there to see you go. *(He has now become emotional, he forms his words with effort)* The rest... I only hope I have understood.

Leggatt *(Also emotional, tearful)* You have. From first to last.

They grasp each other tightly in an embrace.

After a few seconds, they push the map aside, kiss passionately and drop back onto the bed.

Lights snap to blackout.

Act Three - Scene Three

THE QUARTER-DECK OF THE GEMINUS

The light is low, the stage is dark and shadowy. The little light there is has a blueish, silvery glint. All around there is the sound of crashing waves – The sea is wild and violent tonight.

Skeres is at the wheel.

Frizer is winding some rope.

Frizer What sort of captain would risk a ship like this?

Skeres Dolls and toys, that's what we've become. There were a time when women and kids were first in the lifeboats, that was their privilege at sea. Now I'm seeing them given whole ships and their crew's lives to play with.

Frizer And it'll be us that pays the price.

Skeres We're drawing in pretty fast. Land looks horrible close.

Frizer At least we can still see it. That's a luxury we won't have for much longer. The sun's almost deserted us.

Skeres I'm more concerned with what we can't see, sun or no sun.

Frizer Yes, there's a reef in there that will slash our hull like a razor though flesh.

Skeres Suppose we do have a chance, The Geminus is a nimble ship.

Frizer She'll need to be.

Hotson walks out onto the deck slowly. He is dressed in his immaculate shirt and trousers.

Hotson She will weather!

Frizer Are you really going to try this, sir?

Hotson *(Ignoring his question)* Keep her good full.

Skeres Good full, sir.

The sound of the waves becomes more intense, the light even dimmer.

Frizer *(Looking round, his face filled with panic)* Now I can't see the sails, never mind the land. This is madness.

Skeres *(Glancing round at the darkness)* And still not a whisper of a land breeze. Are we going on, sir?

Hotson Keep her full.

Skeres My God! Where are we?

Frizer Lost and damned!

Hotson *(Sternly)* Be quiet!

Frizer *(Dashing about, panicking)* She'll never get out. You've done it, you blasted fool. I knew it'd all end in some calamity. She'll never weather this, we're too close to stay. We're on the reef – gutted on the rocks. Oh my God!

Hotson grabs Frizer's arm.

Hotson Stop it, man!

Frizer We're sunk, we're dead, we're already in the darkest hell.

Hotson *(Shaking Frizer)* Are we? *(Over his shoulder to Skeres)* Keep good full there!

Skeres *(His voice trembling)* Good full, sir!

Frizer *(Pointing)* You're sailing us right into the gate of everlasting night, look at it!

Hotson *(Continuing to shake Frizer)* That's just the

dark shadow of the southern hill of Koh-ring, man!

Frizer How can a shadow be the Devil's doorway? I'm stopping you, I must stop you!

Frizer pulls himself free of Hotson's grip. He runs over to Skeres and attempts to drag him away from the ship's wheel. They struggle.

Skeres is thrown aside, he hits the deck hard and lies there dazed.

Frizer takes the wheel. He begins to turn it frantically.

Hotson runs over and pulls him away. They struggle. They exchange punches, blows, headbutts.

Skeres recovers and gets to his feet. He grabs back onto the wheel.

Now Hotson has his hands around Frizer's throat. He begins to throttle him. He pushes Frizer to his knees and squeezes.

Leggatt emerges from his hiding place. He climbs from the stage and begins to walk the central aisle.

Frizer is making a horrible choking sound, his tongue out, his eyes wide.

Hotson continues to press his fingers into Frizer's

throat. But then he catches sight of Leggatt walking away.

Leggatt turns, he and Hotson make eye contact.

Frizer's falls silent, his body limp.

Hotson looks down at Frizer and realises what he's doing. He relaxes his grip and lets Frizer slump to the deck.

Frizer groans and rolls onto his back. He's alive.

Hotson *(Loudly over his shoulder)* See the head-sheets are properly overhauled. *(Turning to Skeres)* Ready about, do you hear? We go on.

Skeres *(In a meek, worried voice)* Sir?

Hotson *(Steady and confidant)* I know this is the right course. I am confident in that. I feel it in this ship beneath my feet, I feel it in the nature of the sea all about us.

Leggatt continues to walk until he has vanished.

Frizer rolls about on the deck, grasping his throat, clearly still in pain.

Skeres Ha! She's pulling forward, the ship's gathered sternaway. We've caught the land breeze.

Hotson *(Shouting over his shoulder)* Shift the helm!

Frizer gets to his feet, a look of relief and amazement on his face. One hand still at his throat.

Skeres She's round, we've done it. *(Calling over his shoulder)* Let go and haul.

Skeres looks at Hotson, they smile and then nod respectfully at each other.

Hotson I'll take the wheel, Skeres.

Hotson takes the wheel.

Skeres We're safe and heading home. Well done, sir.

Skeres walks off and exits.

Frizer also nods at Hotson, nervously, ashamed. Then he skulks off, his head hung and exits.

Hotson looks ahead, holding onto the ship's wheel as the lights slowly dim to blackout.

End.

BY THE SAME AUTHOR

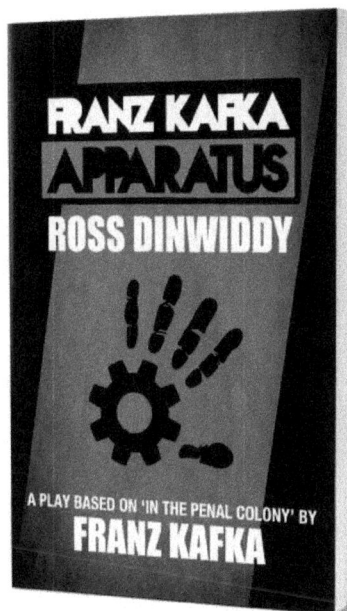

www.ingramcontent.com/pod-product-compliance
Lightning Source LLC
Chambersburg PA
CBHW071020040426
42443CB00007B/864